MILES DAVIS

Jazz Musician and Composer

Celebrating BLACK ARTISTS

MILES DAVIS

Jazz Musician and Composer

CHARLOTTE ETINDE-CROMPTON AND
SAMUEL WILLARD CROMPTON

Enslow Publishing
101 W. 23rd Street
Suite 240
New York, NY 10011
USA
enslow.com

Published in 2020 by Enslow Publishing, LLC
101 W. 23rd Street, Suite 240, New York, NY 10011

Library of Congress Cataloging-in-Publication Data

Names: Etinde-Crompton, Charlotte, author. | Crompton, Samuel Willard, author.
Title: Miles Davis : jazz musician and composer / Charlotte Etinde-Crompton and Samuel Willard Crompton.
Description: New York, NY : Enslow Publishing, 2020. | Series: Celebrating black artists | Audience: Grade 7-12. | Includes bibliographical references and index.
Identifiers: LCCN 2019004361| ISBN 9781978514744 (library bound) | ISBN 9781978514737 (pbk.)
Subjects: LCSH: Davis, Miles—Juvenile literature. | Jazz musicians—United States—Biography—Juvenile literature. | Composers—United States—Biography—Juvenile literature.
Classification: LCC ML3930.D33 E75 2020 | DDC 788.9/2165092 [B] —dc23
LC record available at https://lccn.loc.gov/2019004361

Printed in the United States of America

To Our Readers: We have done our best to make sure all website addresses in this book were active and appropriate when we went to press. However, the author and the publisher have no control over and assume no liability for the material available on those websites or on any websites they may link to. Any comments or suggestions can be sent by email to customerservice@enslow.com.

Photo Credits: Miles Davis – Photo Research by Bruce Donnola

Cover, p. 3 Gilles Petard/Redferns/Getty Images; p. 8 Keystone/Hulton Archive/Getty Images; pp. 10, 56-57, 65, 69 Michael Ochs Archives/Getty Images; p. 12 Lipnitzki/Roger Viollet/Getty Images; p. 16 Andre SAS/Gamma-Rapho/Getty Images; pp. 20-21 Bettmann/Getty Images; pp. 24-25 Pictorial Press Ltd/Alamy Stock Photo; p. 28 MCNY/Gottscho-Schleisner/Archive Photos/Getty Images; pp. 31, 32-33, 40 William Gottlieb/Redferns/Getty Images; p. 42 dcphoto/Alamy Stock Photo; p. 46 Ted Williams/Iconic Images/Getty Images; p. 49 Records/Alamy Stock Photo; p. 54 Gai Terrell/Redferns/Getty Images; p. 61 Metronome/Archive Photos/Getty Images; pp. 66-67 EyeBrowz/Alamy Stock Photo; pp. 72-73 Lynn Goldsmith/Corbis Historical/Getty Images; p. 77 Moses Robinson/WireImage/Getty Images; p. 79 Ron Galella Collection/Getty Images; pp. 80-81 Jeff Kravitz/FilmMagic, Inc/Getty Images; pp. 88-89 Christian Bertrand/Shutterstock.com; p. 91 Paul Natkin/Archive Photos/Getty Images

Contents

Chapter 1

A Prophet Without Honor

Jazz trumpeter and bandleader Miles Davis was the ultimate rebel. He shattered ideas about jazz music and defied the expectations that others imposed on him. Throughout his decades-long musical career, he bucked trends and established his own. And much to the surprise of critics, his music appealed to both black and white listeners. At his best, Miles Davis was "the king of cool," but that is hardly the whole story.

Davis could be temperamental and sometimes downright abusive. While his fans overlooked his sins, a string of wives and girlfriends did not. Davis believed that being a great artist allowed him to behave however he wanted in his private life, but this sense of entitlement caused all sorts of problems for him and his loved ones. Still, Davis remained unapologetic about his conduct right up to his death in 1991. The result has been that many people admire his music but not the man himself.

The Parisian Take on Jazz

While addiction, abuse allegations, and broken relationships haunted Miles Davis in his final years, he began his career

An aerial view of the Eiffel Tower, with the River Seine on the left, circa 1953. This is the structure for which Paris is best known. Miles Davis would have seen it and other landmarks during his visit to the city.

as a fresh-faced jazz artist with no reputation to precede him other than his musical skills. In 1949, a twenty-two-year-old Davis visited what many considered to be the world's hippest city—Paris. The French capital looked dim and dingy in the aftermath of World War II, which had ended just four years earlier. But Americans and other visitors felt drawn to the city because of the lifestyle there.

Parisians were grateful to have survived World War II, which killed tens of millions of people. They made it a priority to enjoy life in the present. That meant indulging in high culture and the good life, especially the arts. In this context, the City of Light, as Paris is known, hosted the International Festival of Jazz in the spring of 1949. The event attracted a number of Americans, including a dashing Miles Davis.

Even before the young musician set foot in Paris, he managed to create buzz. Local musicians heard that he was talented, and Boris Vian, a well-connected jazz artist there, wrote an essay about him for *Jazz News*, published in time for the festival.

"The first thing that strikes you about Miles Davis is that he's really beautiful to look at," Vian wrote.[1] An American essayist might have been too embarrassed to comment on Davis's beauty, but Boris Vian was not. The bleak postwar atmosphere, which had not entirely disappeared, led Parisians to celebrate beauty in all its forms. "People tell me he's too short but that's a meaningless quibble," Vian asserted.[2]

Vian was just the first of dozens of essayists and biographers to comment on Miles Davis's height. The musician was 5 feet 7 inches (170 centimeters) tall, just a

As a young musician, Miles Davis possessed good looks and a boyish charm that would fade as drug addiction and a number of personal problems caught up with him.

couple of inches shorter than the average American male. But on both sides of the Atlantic Ocean, African American men had been stereotyped as towering figures. Historically in the United States, this generalization of black men had been used to frame them as threats to white society, particularly to white women. Yet Miles Davis, and scores of other black men, did not fit this stereotype. Rather, his boyish looks and slight physique reminded Vian of a young deer.

"And though I'm not sure you can trust photographs in general, in one of them he appears to have the ears of a fawn, which I find really nice," he said.[3]

Davis's expressive face led people to sense his inner power. But beyond his looks, Vian was most interested in the American's distinct approach to jazz. Parisians considered the art form the finest to surface from the United States, and Vian thought Davis had a unique approach to the genre. He found the musician's jazz both relaxing and reassuring, likening it to Davis "saunter[ing] in through a flower garden in the month of May."[4]

Here, too, Miles Davis stood out. Europeans were used to hearing bold jazz music that attempted to bowl over its audience. At the time, Charlie Parker and Dizzy Gillespie were both top jazz artists, as was Duke Ellington. But in Davis, the jazz world found a musician who played the music in a careful and intentional manner instead of in an explosive way.[5]

Davis had a sound best described as spare or even "totally calm," as Vian put it.[6] Before he had arrived in Paris, Miles Davis had made an impression, and a spectacular one at that.

Man About Town

Boris Vian might have been a huge admirer of Davis, but many artists in the Parisian jazz scene did not share his views. They thought Vian had overstated the case about Davis. Sure, the young American might have had talent, they said, but his sound was hardly as unique as the critic made it out to be.

French writer and philosopher Jean-Paul Sartre at the Antoine Theater in Paris, France, in November 1946. He enjoyed getting to know Miles Davis.

Back home in New York City, Miles Davis was completely unaware that Parisians were debating his music. Although he was very young, he lived a rather quiet life. He lived with his high school sweetheart and their two children. He had also never taken an airplane flight. His gig at the International Jazz Festival would change that, of course. Once the time came for him to head abroad, Davis was

The Existentialists

Jean-Paul Sartre was born June 21, 1905, in Paris, France. He was the most famous of the existentialists, a group of philosophers who speculated on the absurdity of modern life. Sartre was a leader of the movement that asserted the modern world had stripped humans of their humanness. His longtime partner, the feminist and philosopher Simone de Beauvoir, was also part of this group.

In addition to philosophy, Sartre wrote novels, plays, and literary criticism, but American readers did not take to him right away. In the optimistic postwar period, the US public looked for cheerier viewpoints than his work offered. But Sartre became more important to American readers once they became disillusioned by the Vietnam War during the late 1960s and early 1970s. Today, the works of Sartre and Beauvoir are still influential and widely taught in US colleges and universities.

Sartre died in 1980 at age seventy-four.

thrilled to leave the United States behind. In Paris, he found people who believed in his talent despite the fact that he was a black man. In America, often the opposite occurred; a person's skin color led people to dismiss one's talent.

With his new environment to bolster him, Davis played wonderfully at the International Jazz Festival. And as he wandered around the city, he drew lots of attention. Parisians were taken with the gifted black musician. Boris Vian, predictably, was one of them. He became fast friends with Davis after introducing himself to the American. Vian was a talented and influential person himself. He knew not only musicians but also almost everyone in the Paris arts scene—from poets to filmmakers to novelists. Thanks to Vian, Davis met France's best-known public intellectual, Jean-Paul Sartre.

At first glance, it might seem that these two had little in common. But Sartre was a competent pianist and had more than a passing interest in jazz. The philosopher, however, was far more interested in differences than similarities, and he perceived Davis to be quite different. He wanted to know more about this exceptionally talented American of color who had more of a following in Europe than he did in the United States.

Davis also took an interest in Sartre. The musician was no expert on philosophy but familiar enough with the topic to discuss it with the master. Then, someone introduced Davis to the French actress and singer Juliette Gréco, and Davis was immediately smitten with her. All thoughts of philosophy and music left his mind, and he decided to romantically pursue her, despite the fact that he was a father of two in a long-term relationship.

Love at First Sight

Is there such a thing? This question has been posed countless times, even by respected figures such as South African statesman Nelson Mandela. Before becoming South Africa's president, Mandela fought against apartheid, or racial segregation, in his country. He spent years in prison for his activism. Yet Mandela is also known for his longtime marriage to Winnie Mandela. When he first saw Winnie Mandela on a commuter train, he silently declared that she would one day be his wife.

For Miles Davis, the attraction to Juliette Gréco felt extremely powerful as well. But she was a beautiful woman, and he was a man in a serious relationship. Love likely isn't the accurate word to describe his response to the French performer. For those people who believe that love is an action, or a series of actions over time, what Davis felt for Gréco was certainly not love. Passion is probably a better description of his reaction to her.

Born on mainland France, Gréco is of Corsican heritage. (Corsica is a Mediterranean island that's part of France but remains culturally Italian.) Now in her nineties, she was an active figure in the French Resistance during World War II, and she quickly became a hero to the modern intellectuals of postwar Paris. Blessed with great beauty, she also had a quick mind.

Miles Davis poses with the French actress and singer Juliette Gréco, with whom he had a brief but passionate love affair while in Paris.

While it's clear that Davis felt drawn to Gréco, it's not certain exactly how she reacted to him. The pair spent many hours together, though, and the Paris tabloids followed them from one street corner to another. Before long, the ten-day period Davis was scheduled to be in Paris was up, and he had to return to his predictable and middle-class lifestyle in the United States.

Chapter 2

An Unhappy Childhood

Miles Dewey Davis III was born May 26, 1926, in Alton, Illinois, to Miles Davis II and Cleota Henry Davis. He was the second of three children in an upper-middle-class family and received the message early on that he needed to do something substantial in life, just as his father and grandfather had.

Early Years

Miles's grandfather, who owned a large farm in Missouri, had excelled as a farmer and bookkeeper. And Miles's father also become a successful farmer who was determined to go far in life. Lacking a high school diploma, he passed an equivalency test and soon became a dentist, an occupation in which few black men found themselves at the time. Both he and Miles's mother enjoyed playing music, though neither tried to perform professionally.

"My father got out of Northwestern [University Dental School] and married my mother," Miles later recalled. "She played the violin and the piano. Her mother had been an organ teacher in Arkansas. She never talked much about

The First African American Dentists

The first African Americans to practice dentistry in the United States can be traced to the period following the Civil War. In 1869, Robert Tanner Freeman and George Franklin Grant graduated from Harvard University to become the nation's earliest professionally trained black dentists.

Achieving this goal wasn't easy. Many universities at this time excluded black people from admission, and Harvard and two other schools had turned down Freeman's application because of his race. A Harvard dean fought for Freeman's enrollment at the university, arguing that it was time for the institution to stop excluding students based on skin color.

Freeman and Grant belonged to Harvard's inaugural class of dental students. Just fourteen other students had this distinction. Grant went on to teach in Harvard's department of mechanical dentistry, making him the university's first black professor. Freeman returned to his native Washington, DC, to practice dentistry, but he died in 1873 from a water-borne disease. Grant died in 1910 of liver disease.[1]

her father, so I don't know much about her side of the family ... From what I have heard of them, though, and the ones I did meet, they seemed to be middle class and a little uppity in their attitudes."[2]

When Miles was a toddler, the Davises moved from Alton to East St. Louis, Illinois. Miles recalled that his first memory was watching a blue flame jumping off a gas stove. "I remember being shocked by the whoosh of the blue flame jumping off the burner, the suddenness of it," he remembered years later. "That stove flame is as clear as music is in my mind. I was three years old."[3] The flame marked the first time the little boy felt real fear, and his reaction made him feel excited and joyful at the same time. "I guess that experience took me somewhere in my head I hadn't been before," he recalled.[4]

In East St. Louis, the Davises started out humbly but quickly settled in a middle-class neighborhood. Miles's father was extremely ambitious, and he soon purchased a large country farm on the outskirts of town. It was about 200 acres (80 hectares), which allowed Miles to

In 1917, East St. Louis endured a race riot that claimed up to 250 black people's lives. The racial tensions hadn't entirely dissipated when Miles Davis and his family moved there.

grow up riding horses. With lots of land and a dentist father, Miles may have been more privileged than many boys his age, but his parents had a rocky marriage that made his home life hard to bear. He often felt lost and abandoned, especially by his mother, whose face he remembered as being cold and hard.

Miles's parents frequently quarreled—sometimes to the point of violence. On one occasion, his mother hurled a heavy pot at her husband's head but narrowly missed striking her target. Miles's father did not share his wife's temper, but he was emotionally distant. He often spent long hours on the job, away from his wife and children.

To some extent, Miles and his siblings—his older sister, Dorothy Mae, and his younger brother, Vernon—raised each other. They shielded each other from their parents' conflicts and tried to make a normal life for themselves. But Miles doubted that his family could ever be normal, so he decided to embrace being different. The horses on the family farm offered an escape. Miles felt a special bond with the animals, and it deepened when his father gifted him one as a birthday present.

A Budding Musician

Young Miles also found solace in music. No one knows exactly when he first picked up an instrument, but we do know that his mother gave him a violin for his birthday. His father, however, disapproved and gave him a trumpet to play instead. That instrument seemed perfect for Davis, who was short and small for his age.

Miles was not the only child in his family who enjoyed music. His siblings appreciated the art form as well, and their interest added joy to their turbulent home environment. Davis later explained:

> All of us kids—my brother and my sister and me—liked artistic things when we were young … So, I would play trumpet—as much as I could play back then—and Dorothy would play piano, Vernon would dance. We had a lot of fun … Mostly we would do little skits … with me being the judge.[5]

Miles didn't just play music around the house for fun but took formal lessons in piano, violin, and trumpet. While formally studying music certainly helped his development as an artist, he credited informal tutoring with giving him the foundation needed to become a remarkable musician. Growing up in East St. Louis also influenced Miles, as the city was a center for music in the 1930s. There, he spent time on street corners and in dive bars to hear the latest genres.

Miles's interest in music interfered with his studies. While he earned good marks, he didn't earn great ones. His teachers recognized his intelligence, especially his analytical mind, but lamented that he spent so much time on music. The teen often missed the opening moments of school because he listened to *Harlem Rhythms*, a well-known jazz program that aired at 8:30 a.m.

In 1941, Miles endured the breakup of his parents' marriage. In the months leading up to World War II, the differences between husband and wife became too profound to ignore. His father moved into a house a few miles away, and the three Davis children felt lost. They sympathized with their father while craving their mother's

Jazz artist Jelly Roll Morton (*seated at the piano*) and his backing band. Artists like Morton changed music a great deal during Miles Davis's youth, and Davis himself would grow up to be a jazz trendsetter.

Ragtime and Jazz

East St. Louis, Illinois, and neighboring St. Louis, Missouri, are associated with ragtime, the buoyant musical genre that began to gain popularity in the late 1800s and early 1900s. The African American musician Scott Joplin is known for pioneering this form of music, named for its "ragged," or slightly off-beat, rhythms. Joplin's works such as the "Maple Leaf Rag" and "The Entertainer" helped to earn him the nickname the "King of Ragtime."

By the time Miles Davis had reached his teenage years in the 1940s, interest in ragtime had faded, and East St. Louis also had the distinction of being a center for jazz. The adolescent had the good fortune to grow up less than a mile away from some of the most exciting new sounds in the American Midwest. And the music he was exposed to in his early years would influence him throughout his career.

love, but they seldom received it. In the past, the Davis children had depended on each other to survive their parents' dysfunctional relationship. By their teen years, however, each of the siblings felt truly alone.

But Miles had found a way to persevere. Music was his refuge. "When I got into music, I went all the way into music," he said. "I didn't have no time after that for nothing else."[6]

Chapter 3

Jazz at a Crossroads

For years, jazz was like a freight train, continually headed in one direction. The early experimentation of the 1920s led the genre to stabilize in the 1930s. And World War II, which began in 1939, only helped jazz become more popular. Tens of thousands of soldiers heard jazz for the first time during the war, and some became lifelong fans. But as jazz took over the music industry, the freight train split into two and headed in different directions.

Life in the Big Apple

Miles Davis was only fifteen when the United States entered World War II. He was too young to influence the direction of jazz but old enough to observe new music trends. He caught on to them and never let them go.

Just three years later, however, Miles's life changed dramatically. He was no longer an unattached teenager free to come and go as he pleased but a young man with a family. It all happened rather suddenly. Miles began to take a mild interest in girls in his mid-teens, even dating a much-admired student named Irene Cawthon. Irene was two years older than Miles and made him just as popular as she was. The two became inseparable, and even though Miles's parents disapproved, he ignored them. Because of their divorce and extremely unhealthy marriage, Miles no longer respected their opinions. When the underage Miles asked for their permission to marry his girlfriend, they withheld their consent. But Miles started living with her anyway. They soon had a son named Gregory. For Miles,

Miles Davis wasn't particularly interested in attending college, but to please his mother, he enrolled in the Juilliard School and made a life for himself in New York City.

becoming an adult also meant leaving behind East St. Louis. His mother wanted him to attend Fisk University in Nashville, Tennessee, where his big sister had gone. But Miles had his eyes set firmly on New York City, particularly the Juilliard School of Music, where he headed after his 1944 high school graduation.

Going to Juilliard was a compromise of sorts between Miles and his mother. Although he didn't go to Fisk, her first choice, deciding to attend college at all was a way of placating her. Higher education really didn't interest Miles, but in Juilliard, he found an institution that would allow him to focus on music. In September 1944, Miles arrived in New York, the pace of which amazed him. "I thought St. Louis and Chicago were fast, but they weren't anything like New York City," he later recalled. "So, that was the first thing I had to get used to, all the people. But getting around by subway was a gas, it was so fast."[1]

Davis was "wet behind the ears," meaning he was young and inexperienced, especially when it came to a huge city such as New York.[2] Still, he quickly caught on to his new environment. Before long, he had a room at the Claremont Hotel on Riverside Drive, and he passed his entrance exams to Juilliard. Financial assistance from his dentist father allowed the teenager to start out his life in New York this way. His dad paid Miles's Juilliard tuition and room and board. He also provided $40 monthly for entertainment expenses. Today, that would be the equivalent of roughly $580.

With a comfortable new life in the Big Apple, Miles focused on the city's music scene. Back in East St. Louis, he'd learned to play the trumpet so well that he already

Dizzy Gillespie

Born October 21, 1917, in Cheraw, South Carolina, Dizzy Gillespie was a composer and trumpeter who became a jazz bandleader. His father was an amateur musician who introduced young Dizzy to various instruments. But when his father died in 1927, Dizzy figured out how to play the trumpet and trombone on his own. He went on to take music classes at the Laurinburg Institute in North Carolina.

Gillespie played in several bands in the 1930s and 1940s and had the good fortune to perform with jazz greats such as Cab Calloway, Ella Fitzgerald, and Duke Ellington. He could have made a great living playing the old-style jazz that flourished in the late 1930s. Instead, he ushered in a new jazz movement known as bebop.

In 1944, Gillespie recorded his first bebop number. Bebop is a form of jazz characterized by a fast tempo and exciting chord changes. Gillespie had many hits over the years, including "Woody 'n' You," "Salt Peanuts," "Groovin' High," and "A Night in Tunisia."

He died on January 6, 1993, at age seventy-five.

Dizzie Gillespie was a pioneer of the bebop sound. Here he is in a 1948 portrait shot with his horn.

The Charlie Parker Quintet, including Parker on saxophone and Miles Davis on trumpet, perform at Three Deuces in New York in August 1947.

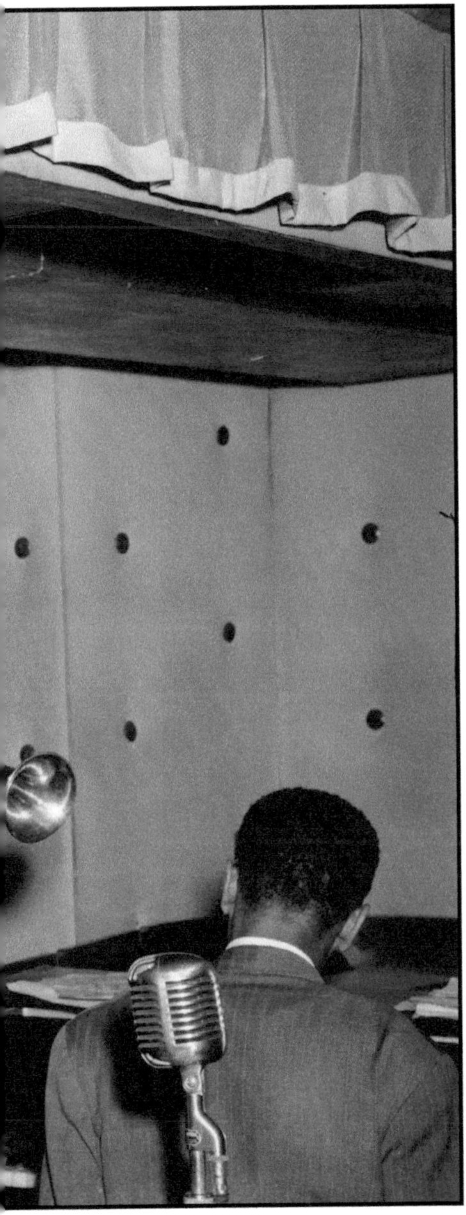

made a decent living from his musical skills. But East St. Louis was no New York. The largest city in the nation attracted the best and brightest musicians from around the country, and Miles yearned to break into the prestigious Manhattan jazz scene. He also longed to meet the jazz players he idolized, such as Dizzy Gillespie and Charlie Parker.

Born in 1920 in Kansas City, Kansas, Charlie Parker was known for being one of the finest saxophone players in Manhattan. He would prove himself to be an excellent composer of music as well. His personal life was in shambles, however. His talent and good looks simply obscured the fact that he suffered from a serious drug addiction and a long list of other self-defeating behaviors.

To young Miles Davis, though, Parker was a hero. He never forgot meeting "Bird," as the musician was nicknamed, for the first time:

> He was dressed in these baggy clothes that looked like he had been sleeping in them for days. His face was all puffed up, and his eyes were swollen and red. But he was cool, with that hipness … No matter how he looked, bad or near death, he still looked good to me that night.[3]

Parker took an immediate liking to Miles. He acted as an older brother and mentor, but he also took advantage of the relationship, borrowing and sometimes stealing the young man's belongings and pawning them. At first, Miles put up with this behavior, but when his girlfriend, Irene Cawthon, and their son arrived from East St. Louis, he kicked Parker out of the apartment.

Almost everyone Miles met in 1944 believed the teenager had a leg up on the musical competition. His father's wealth enabled him to live well in the big city, and he could afford to choose his friends and supporters. He succeeded in all aspects of life with one major exception—school.

Davis had never been terribly excited about attending Juilliard, even though the faculty had the know-how to help him perfect his craft. Some of his professors were racists, and their bigotry left him disillusioned. They believed African Americans were great musicians but only because of slavery. The blues developed, they said, as enslaved blacks picked cotton on plantations. Miles disagreed with these comments. He pointed out how he grew up in a financially privileged household and enjoyed playing the blues. "My father didn't never pick no cotton, and I didn't wake up this morning sad and start playing the blues," Miles told his professors. "There's more to it than that."[4]

The School of Life

For centuries, artists and critics have debated whether school or experience is more valuable to one's craft. Miles Davis strongly believed that experience mattered more than schooling. The truth likely lies somewhere in the middle. Education and experience are both important in the development of artists and other professionals.

But Miles found himself in unique circumstances when he arrived at Juilliard at eighteen. For one, he aspired to learn a musical genre with African roots at a white institution. While his professors could teach him the technical side of music as well as theory and history, they were not necessarily equipped to teach him about an art form with origins in West Africa. Genres such as blues and jazz simply didn't follow the European approach to music that dominated schools like Juilliard. Improvisation, or creating ideas in the moment rather than following written music, played a key role in black musical genres. It's uncertain if he would have learned this important skill at Juilliard.

In the end, Davis made the choice about his education that best suited him, and he went on to become an influential, world-famous jazz artist.

Miles was right, given that blues music has been traced back to the people of western and central Africa. The genre did, in fact, predate slavery in the United States. This information may not have been well known at the time, however, and Miles found few supporters at Juilliard willing to back up his argument. Throughout his career, he would be asked to comment on the link between race and music. When he became a famous musician, for example, he was asked if blacks are naturally better musicians than whites. His answer played into the racial stereotypes of his day. "It seems like white musicians lag a bit behind the beat," he said.[5]

Almost anyone who knew young Miles Davis recognized that he preferred the school of jazz bars to the refined classrooms of Juilliard. The teenager planned to drop out of the institution, but he could not do so immediately. His father had invested a great deal of money into his education, and Miles did not want to seem ungrateful for his father's contributions to his studies.

Miles managed to perform reasonably well at Juilliard during his first semester, but by the second semester, he was barely hanging on. After eighteen months, he dropped out of college. He didn't understand why he needed higher education to learn about jazz when he could simply walk into New York City's nightclubs and discover all he wanted to know about the art form.

Chapter 4

From Bop to Cool

Today, dropping out of college is often viewed as a failure, but Miles Davis considered his decision to leave Juilliard to be an opportunity. Within weeks of this move, he could be found in all of the popular jazz clubs in Manhattan. About to turn twenty years old, Davis already understood more about jazz's broad appeal than many musicians twice his age.

The Cool Sound

During the 1940s, bop music began to take off in New York. It spread to the rest of the East Coast and then to the West Coast. The genre is hard to categorize, and many listeners simply called the art form "new music." Regardless of its label, the new music could not be mistaken for the old. It lacked the smooth harmonies of big band groups and the rhythm of 1930s jazz. Instead, bop sounded almost harsh.

Davis was not one of the early bop musicians, but he realized the music had potential and experimented with the sound that was shaking up the once placid popular music scene. The fact that his father was financially supporting him gave Davis the chance to devote himself to the music.

Father's Insight

During an *Ebony* magazine interview, Miles Davis II described some of the factors that led his first-born son to become such an amazing musician. He said that generations of Davises had played music.

> By genetics and breeding, Miles is always going to be ahead of his time. Historically, way back into slavery days, the Davises have been musicians and performed classical works in the homes of plantation owners. My father, Miles I, was born six years after Emancipation and forbade me to play music because the only place a Negro could play music then was in barrel houses [bars].[1]

Miles II also recalled how his son had been an excellent musician, even in childhood, but attended racially integrated schools where white faculty members refused to acknowledge his talent. That meant that Miles III often received third-place prizes in music contests in which he should have placed first, his father said.

While he and his child may not have been particularly close in the early years, the pair formed a bond during the younger Davis's adulthood. When Miles II died in 1962, his musician son grieved deeply.

Both of his parents took an interest in his music, and knowing that he had the support of his family gave him confidence. He also knew that if his music career didn't work out, he could return to East St. Louis. But his obvious talent made it clear that he would never need to exercise this option.

In fact, Davis quickly landed a series of part-time gigs playing the trumpet. Dedicated to his craft, he had the energy and drive to succeed in the music industry. Starting in 1946, Davis got a job playing in the band of famous singer Billy Eckstine and learned a great deal from the experience. He traveled to the West Coast, played with incredible musicians, and defined his idea of what made good jazz music. By 1948, he had created his own style, the so-called "cool" sound.

Plenty of previous jazz players had experimented with the "cool" sound, but none made it their signature style. The sound appealed to Davis because he preferred music with fewer notes and scales. He thought it sounded better, or as its name implied, "cooler." By January 1949, Miles Davis mastered the cool sound, making several recordings in the genre with the nine-man band known as the Miles Davis Nonet.

The recordings weren't released for several years, but the album, *Birth of the Cool*, was a key moment in the development of jazz. While Davis did not despise bebop, as some jazz players did, he found its use of sound too overwhelming. The genre left listeners little room to develop their own interpretation of the music. This opposed what Davis aimed to do with the cool sound, a spare style that gave listeners plenty of room to interpret what they

Miles Davis learned a great deal from playing in the band of jazz crooner Billy Eckstine.

heard. His experimentation with this style led to Davis's first recording contracts, as well as a relationship with Bob Weinstock of Prestige Records.

On the surface, Davis's future looked bright. But the early 1950s ushered in a horrible chapter in his life. During this period, he nearly lost everything to his heroin addiction, a problem many musicians had. Drugs and alcohol flowed freely in the scene. Jazz artists began to abuse heroin during and after World War II. Once a proficient musician, Davis began to nod off during rehearsals because of his addiction.

The exact details of his addiction are unknown, but it's clear that it became a serious problem and may have turned deadly. His use of heroin also affected his behavior, leaving him angry, withdrawn, and erratic. But when he was using drugs, Davis didn't think about the consequences of his addiction or ponder his future.

"I don't think nothing about death," he said. "I should have been dead a long time ago. But it missed me when I was on dope. That's why I don't have any fear in my eyes."[2]

Kicking the Habit

Miles Davis II lived in a completely different world from his musician son. He was a Midwestern dentist with a horse farm, while his son made his way in and out of jazz clubs and recording studios, constantly exposed to drugs, alcohol, and other vices. Although the elder Davis led a much quieter life than his son did, he managed to help the young man out of a potentially life-ending crisis.

Miles Davis II knew his son was struggling when the jazz artist drove from New York City to East St. Louis, only to have his car repossessed. The incident took place right on the elder Davis's lawn. Life continued to go downhill once the musician returned to New York. But Miles Davis II couldn't bear to have his son unravel in this way, so he headed to Manhattan to rescue him. One night, he pulled him out of a nightclub and took him back to East St. Louis. He told his son that he had to get clean and sober.

Miles Davis's album *Birth of the Cool* features recordings from 1949 and 1950.

The younger Davis ended up going cold turkey to end the addiction. Abruptly giving up a drug like heroin can be dangerous because the body goes into withdrawal. To kick heroin, Davis locked himself in the upstairs apartment of his father's house for seven days straight. He examined the issues that had contributed to his addiction, such as his lonely childhood, his parents' divorce, and even his efforts to become a successful musician.

Heroin Withdrawal

Heroin is a highly addictive substance, and withdrawing from the drug can be a difficult process. How long it takes to go through withdrawal depends on several factors, including how much heroin a user regularly consumes and for what length of time. Just six to twelve hours after going without heroin, a user may feel the symptoms of withdrawal. Because these symptoms are unpleasant, many users continue to take heroin to avoid them.

Withdrawal symptoms include nausea and vomiting, muscle aches and pains, diarrhea, anxiety, perspiration, and insomnia. While it usually takes about a week for users to go through the first and most painful withdrawal symptoms, other signs of withdrawal, such as depression, anxiety, insomnia, and fatigue, may linger for months afterward. Heroin can also have long-lasting effects on the heart, brain, lungs, and other organs.[3]

Davis compared heroin withdrawal to the flu. While it was an excruciating process, he knew that he would eventually feel better. He endured the process moment by moment, hour by hour, until he felt more like himself again.

Miles Davis was never very good at describing his struggles. In reality, his experience with heroin withdrawal was likely much more challenging than he described it. But the main point is that he did it. After a week of complete isolation, he emerged feeling renewed. This didn't mean he had no desire to use drugs again, but he had made it through acute withdrawal, a process that takes six to seven days.

Chapter 5

A Breakthrough Album

The 1950s are not generally viewed as a time of great cultural advancement. Some scholars and pop culture experts even regard the decade as boring. It marked a time when suburban family life, complete with white picket fences and two-car garages, was framed as a goal. But at the end of the decade, Miles Davis released his 1959 album, *Kind of Blue*.

Jazz was never the same.

Kind of Blue

In the 1950s, Davis was already considered to be one of the finest trumpeters around. He looked for exceptionally talented musicians to play in his band and found many fine artists, especially John Coltrane.

With his band, he recorded *Kind of Blue* in just two days: March 2 and April 22, 1959. The band did little rehearsal before the studio sessions. He believed the music would sound better, more organic, if unrehearsed—and he was spot on.

Jazz trumpeter Miles Davis and legendary saxophonist John Coltrane perform onstage at a concert in 1960 in Chicago, Illinois.

The album includes the opener "So What," in which the horns—meaning the trumpet and saxophones—come in early, pipe to a crescendo, and then back off and soften. The listener feels a rainy day and inspiration that comes from a *lack*, rather than a surplus, of visual stimuli. The words "so what" come through in a number of ways, while the track's theme remains the same.

What did Davis mean by "So What"? On one level, Davis asserts that nothing matters, everything material can be taken away. On the other, he seems to grimly express the need for people to take responsibility for the trivial, or impermanent, things in their life that don't mean much in the long run.

"Freddie Freeloader" is the album's second recording. Coming in at nearly ten minutes, it does not stand out like the opener does. The words of the title do not come through in the music. But the song's sentiment is more than adequate. One feels that Miles Davis has known plenty of Freddie Freeloaders (Charlie Parker among them) and that he feels their pain. He might have even viewed himself as a freeloader to a degree.

"Blue in Green," the third tune, starts slowly. The horns then rise and fall like a geyser before turning into a gentle waterfall. The mood is somber but endowed with a sense of gentle hope. Don't ask for too much, the music seems to say, and your hopes may one day be realized.

Coming in fourth, "All Blues" pulls the listener in through the spare elegance of the music. The horns do not begin to build until the third minute of the eleven-minute track. This is the "Davis sound" in a nutshell. His music

Minimal Music

Miles Davis expertly used a minimal number of notes to produce complex music that engaged the senses of listeners. In addition to sound, his music managed to evoke visuals and tap into a wide range of emotions–from passion to sorrow. His music tickled the senses by giving the audience space to "feel" between notes.

Davis was certainly not jazz music's first "spare" player, but he was the most successful at this technique. His predecessors struggled to find an audience and disappeared from the stage and recording studio as a result. Davis came along at just the right time–the late 1950s–when American jazz audiences were ready for a minimalist presentation.

The minimalist movement in US art gained momentum in the 1960s and remained popular through the 1970s. In fact, by 1970, the term "minimal music" had been coined. With his spare sound, however, Davis had produced such music years before this expression was introduced. Once jazz listeners heard the "Davis sound" they tended to be hooked for life.

doesn't overwhelm listeners but gradually draws them into his world.

Davis was also not afraid to experiment with sounds from other cultures. In the Spanish-influenced "Flamenco Sketches," he carried his band to the next level. Time spent in California gave Davis an appreciation for Spanish music.

The cover of Miles Davis's groundbreaking 1959 album, *Kind of Blue*, sets the tone for the music within.

In "Flamenco Sketches," his tone is lighter and livelier, with a Spanish, even Moorish, feel. The trumpet rises slowly. The piano provides excellent backup, but the horns create the main effect.

A later reissue of *Kind of Blue* also includes an alternate version of "Flamenco Sketches" that has a deeper, lower sound. The horns come in earlier, creating a more somber mood. But the message remains the same: Spanish music, brought to New York by way of California, has much to offer.

Fame

Collectively, the works on *Kind of Blue* led to a sea change in the world of jazz. Just months after its release, the album became one of the most discussed in the world. Even people who weren't jazz aficionados felt compelled to listen to the album and give their take on what many fans had deemed a masterpiece. Audiences wondered how Miles Davis and his band had created such an elegantly spare sound and if, thanks to *Kind of Blue*, the old jazz era was over. As interest in the album soared, so did curiosity about Davis, who suddenly found himself labeled the coolest man on the planet. Not only had he pioneered the "cool sound," but Davis, a sharp dresser, looked cool, too. He was already being described as a legend in his own lifetime. One critic wrote of the musician:

> Possessed of a temper as sensitive as a bottle of nitroglycerin and a matchless melody in his muted trumpet, Miles, at 34, makes an estimated $150,000 yearly, and, for jazz, its most dominant influence since

Miles's Sense of Style

Miles Davis loved fashion, and his unique sense of style still earns him shout-outs in publications such as the *New York Times* and *GQ*. Davis credited his mother as a major sartorial influence. In his autobiography, he describes her mink coats and diamonds. "She was a very glamorous woman who was into all kinds of hats and things, and all my mother's friends seemed just as glamorous to me as she was," he wrote. "She always dressed to kill."[1]

But a number of celebrities also influenced his style, which he described as a "hip, quasi-black English look" made up of "Brooks Brothers suits, butcher boy shoes, high top pants, shirts with high tab collars."[2] Actor Cary Grant, dancer Fred Astaire, and jazzmen Coleman Hawkins and Dexter Gordon were all sartorial inspirations for Davis.

"Dexter hipped me to the importance of looking sharp," Davis recalled. "I thought he was the cleanest cat around."[3]

African Americans in and outside of the jazz scene thought it was important to dress their best in a society that judged them for their skin color. Dressing fashionably sent the message that they deserved respect.

> the passing of Charlie Parker. On both sides of the Atlantic, he has won so many jazz polls, the very idea strikes him as stale, and some of his major awards, Miles Davis has never even bothered to pick up.[4]

Davis's lack of interest in awards might have seemed strange to the public, but he likely decided that such honors were superficial when he was growing up in East St. Louis and given third place for performances for which he should have placed first. To fans unfamiliar with this history, however, the jazz artist's disinterest in awards made him all the cooler. In fact, to some, Miles Davis was simply "the man."[5]

Chapter 6

Top of the World

In 1959, Miles Davis was jazz music's most famous artist. His immense talent challenged the idea that African Americans were less skillful musicians than their white counterparts. While his music earned him the respect of fans from all over the world, he was still a black man in America. That meant clashes with policemen who were prone to target African Americans who defied racial stereotypes. With his Ferraris and pricey designer wardrobe, Miles Davis appeared too flashy to some policemen's liking. They did not fawn over him, as they might have done with a white celebrity. Instead, they would pull him over for driving a sportscar or rough him up simply for standing on a sidewalk.

Clash with the Cops

A few months after recording *Kind of Blue*, Miles Davis stood outside a nightclub on 52nd Street. This was a normal hangout for Davis, who often played inside the local club. But on this particular evening, Davis lounged too close to the curb, and two white policemen asked him to move. "Move on, for what?" he replied. "I'm working downstairs. That's my name up there, Miles Davis." He then pointed to the marquee where his name appeared in lights.[1]

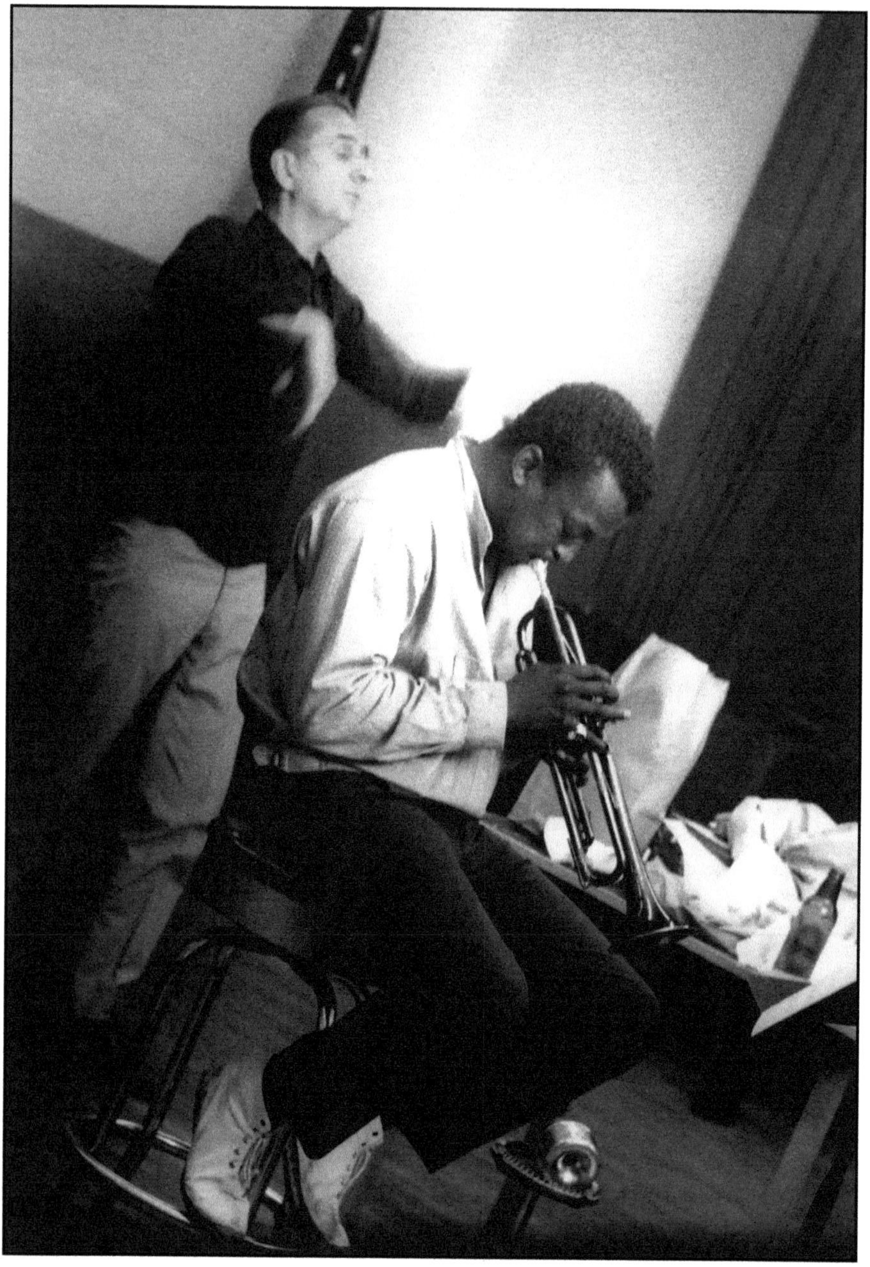

Jazz pianist and bandleader Gil Evans and Miles Davis rehearse for a Carnegie Hall concert on May 1, 1961.

But the officers didn't care that he worked at the club; they threatened to arrest him if he didn't move. And before he knew it, a white detective hit him on the head, according to Davis. In his memoir, he recalled the traumatic event:

> It was almost a race riot, so the police got scared and hurried up and got … out of there and took me to the 54th Precinct where they took pictures of me bleeding … I would have expected this kind of bullshit about resisting arrest and all back in

Losing One's Voice

Miles Davis's violent encounter with New York City police wasn't the only time his physical health was put at risk in the 1950s. Two years before the incident at the nightclub, the trumpeter underwent surgery for a possible cancerous growth in the throat. His physician warned him not to use his voice for at least ten days afterward, but Davis ignored this advice.

Disregarding the doctor's orders had lifelong consequences for the musician. It resulted in him speaking with a low rasp, which put off many people. The macho Davis found it especially annoying that his voice was routinely mistaken for a woman's on the telephone. Fortunately for the musician, his botched recovery from surgery did not affect his jazz career. Careful listeners can almost always pick out the distinct sound of Miles Davis on the trumpet.

East St. Louis (before the city went all-black), but not here in New York City, which is supposed to be the slickest, hippest city in the world.[2]

American composer, pianist, and bandleader Duke Ellington. Ellington's success and fame paved the way for later artists like Davis.

Davis was later cleared of the charges the policemen had filed against him, but the incident lingered with him and his millions of fans. A photo of Davis taken the night of the beating shows his tie, shirt, and blazer covered in splotches of blood. If the cops were willing to pummel a famous musician like Miles Davis in liberal Manhattan, was any African American really safe from police brutality? The black community pondered this question after Davis's beating and arrest.

This violent encounter with police certainly marked a low point for Davis, but he would continue to celebrate highs in his career. The music of a foreign country would lead to more praise for the jazz star.

Sketches of Spain

With the *Kind of Blue* track "Flamenco Sketches," Davis revealed his interest in classical Spanish music to the world. In 1960, he followed up that single with *Sketches of Spain*, considered his finest international work to date. While the album did not cover much ground, musically speaking, it was considered a breakthrough for an American musician to wholly embrace the rhythm and culture of a foreign nation.

When *Sketches of Spain* debuted in the summer of 1960, it proved to be excellent timing. Americans were taking more of an interest in Spain and Latin America as the number of Latino immigrants in the United States began to rise. Arranged by Gil Evans, who had already lent his genius to *Birth of the Cool*, *Sketches* transported the modern jazz listener to rural Spain. The album starts with "Concierto de Aranjuez," which conjures up images and sounds, such as the rumble of carts on the town's streets. The album also includes "Will o' the Wisp," a shorter and punchier tune with a dreamlike quality.

Additionally, *Sketches of Spain* features "The Pan Piper," a traditional Spanish song that speaks to the relationship between loneliness, hopelessness, and fearlessness. "Pan Piper" is followed by "Saeta," a Spanish religious song, and "Salea," a form of flamenco music. *Sketches of Spain* stands out in how it brought the European nation to life for American audiences. A number of jazz greats, including Duke Ellington, had performed all over the world, but Davis brought a slice of the world to his American fans.

Breaking Up the Band

Miles Davis felt like he was on top of the world in 1960. Unfortunately, he did not stay there long. Losing a talented member from his band, now a quintet, sent him crashing back down to Earth.

Most of the musicians in his band felt grateful to perform with him. They did not complain about the long hours or the pay. They knew Davis was a true master and believed that their work with him would pay off. But Davis was not easy to work for, as he drove himself and his band members hard.

The musician played through injuries and pain and had little patience for artists who weren't as dedicated to their craft as he was. As the 1960s began, some of his

John Coltrane

John Coltrane was born on September 23, 1926, in Hamlet, North Carolina. The same age as Miles Davis, Coltrane saw his musical career take off during the same period: the 1940s and 1950s. He became a master saxophonist and composer. In addition to performing in Davis's band, Coltrane played with the jazz giants Dizzy Gillespie and Duke Ellington.

Coltrane has been described as a jazz innovator and virtuoso. *Giant Steps*, *My Favorite Things*, and *A Love Supreme* are a few of the albums that feature his remarkable playing.

He died from complications of liver cancer on July 17, 1967, in Huntington, New York. He was forty years old.[3]

hardworking bandmates wanted out. They wondered if another bandleader would be more generous or less demanding than Davis was. Among these musicians was John Coltrane, arguably the most talented of the group. The legendary saxophonist left the band in 1960, a huge loss for Miles Davis. His work never sounded quite the same after Coltrane's departure, many of his fans said.

Chapter 7

The Sixties

On the surface, the 1960s seem to be Miles Davis's decade. Davis had the talent and public persona to thrive during this difficult period. But Davis found, much to his own surprise, that the musical world was ready to move on from him.

Transitions

Davis was always ambivalent about rock music. Had he been born a decade later, he might well have become one of the great rock showmen. But he came of age, musically, when jazz was at its peak, and it was too late for Davis to reinvent himself. As rock became the nation's dominant music, however, the jazz artist still enjoyed some successes.

George Avakian, the musical director at Columbia Records, had great faith in Davis and his music. But with each passing year, it grew harder to find and keep the right musicians. Davis did not micromanage his musicians' lives, and he allowed for their eccentricities and excesses, which he had plenty of himself. As he became more famous,

Jazz arranger and pianist Billy Strayhorn (*left*) and jazz producer and critic George Avakian listen to Duke Ellington, who sits at the keyboard.

however, the musicians in his band found it hard to accept their relatively low pay for performing with him. The fame and the riches all seemed to go to Davis.

It's not exactly clear why Davis didn't increase the pay of his band members. He was not a greedy man. In fact, he did not care much about money, but he did like what he could get with it—fancy clothes, flashy sportscars, and the attention of beautiful women. He drove a yellow Ferrari around the streets of Manhattan, attracting not only women but police officers as well. Davis later claimed that police pulled him over on an almost weekly basis. In the 1960s, few men, black or white, earned enough money to drive an Italian sportscar.

Behind the money and the success, Davis hid his emotional state. He tended to behave as if he hadn't a care in the world, even when he was personally struggling. The women in his life, however, got to see the insecure, and abusive, side of the trumpeter. More devoted to jazz than to Irene Cawthon and his three children with her, Davis had parted ways with his high school sweetheart. By the late 1950s, he was dating a dancer named Frances Taylor. The two wed in December 1960.[1]

But the couple certainly didn't have a fairytale marriage. Filled with jealousy, rage, and abuse, it was the exact opposite. Davis was so controlling that he insisted his wife, who'd gotten a part in the film version of the musical *West Side Story*, drop out of the project. He practically kept her a prisoner in their glamorous Manhattan apartment, all the while cheating on her with various women. Moreover, he seemed to fear that her

The Controlling Person

On the stage or set, Miles Davis was frequently rude to his audience. But at home, he was much worse. He had to control everything and everyone. Where did this overwhelming insecurity come from?

Psychologists naturally point to Davis's youth, when his parents were constantly at odds with each other. The divorce had also deeply affected him and made him feel alone. But many Americans grow up in dysfunctional families. This experience does not mean that the children in these families will be abusive adults.

Davis used drugs and alcohol, and dependence on these substances can lead addicts to have angry outbursts and be downright cruel. But Davis didn't just have a nasty temper; he physically abused the women in his life, behavior that's never acceptable, no matter the cause.

entertainment career would take off, perhaps even eclipsing his own.

"There could not be two stars in that family," Taylor later recalled. Davis had to be the superstar, and his wife came along for the ride. Davis *had* to be in charge. He admitted this in an interview many years later. In 1968, the couple split. The very same year, he married Betty Mabry, a model nineteen years his junior.

Exploring Rock 'n' Roll

Miles Davis rarely admired another person's music. When subjected to blindfold tests—in which he listened to other performers without knowing their names—he tended to hand out average grades. Occasionally, he handed out an outright failing one. But Davis found a select few musicians

Jimi Hendrix

Jimi Hendrix was born November 27, 1942, in Seattle, Washington. In his teens, he learned to play guitar, and by his twenties, he was electrifying audiences with his showmanship. He played backup guitar for music legends such as Little Richard, B. B. King, Sam Cooke, and the Isley Brothers before becoming famous in his own right. In 1966, he formed the Jimi Hendrix Experience and churned out hits with the group, such as "Hey Joe," "Purple Haze," and "The Wind Cries Mary." His performance of "The Star-Spangled Banner" at 1969's Woodstock music festival is one of his most well known.

He died from a drug overdose on September 18, 1970, in London, England. He was twenty-seven years old and is considered a member of the "27 Club." This is a reference to the fact that several musicians, including Jim Morrison, Janis Joplin, Kurt Cobain, and Amy Winehouse, have died at age twenty-seven.[2]

impressive, among them Jimi Hendrix, to whom he'd been introduced by his wife Betty.

The rock star thrilled audiences while jamming on his electric guitar. Miles Davis, who shrugged at other musicians' efforts, was a Hendrix fan. He hoped to work with the guitarist and vocalist, but Hendrix overdosed on drugs before Davis got the opportunity to collaborate with him.

Rock guitarist Jimi Hendrix poses for a portrait in 1966 in London, England. Miles Davis found his music inspirational and wanted to collaborate with him.

The stunning cover of Miles Davis's vinyl album *Bitches Brew*. The album was released in 1970.

Though the two never got to work together, Hendrix's mark can be clearly felt on Davis's 1970 album, *Bitches Brew*. The album was inspired by rock music as well as Betty Mabry and her friends. The couple had divorced in 1969 but continued to see each other, and she is said to have heavily influenced his new taste in music. *Bitches Brew* marked a shift for Davis, not only musically but also visually. Over the years, Davis had already experimented with a variety of album covers, but the art *Bitches Brew* featured was unlike any he'd chosen previously. The cover art includes a face resembling Davis's in the upper left corner, and two scantily clad women in tribal garb appear at the bottom. Their backs to the viewer, they fold arms, embellished with gold bands. Fire, lightning, and the ocean can be seen behind the two figures. They represent a musical style known as jazz fusion, in which jazz is mixed with elements from other genres, such as funk and rock.

Chapter 8

Hard Times

Miles Davis fans were not pleased with *Bitches Brew*. Many accused him of abandoning his jazz roots. But newcomers, those too young to remember *Birth of the Cool* and *Kind of Blue*, were blown away. Here was a jazz master who could incorporate rock 'n' roll into his music, they said. Astonishingly, Davis was only forty-four years old. He had played with Dizzy Gillespie and Charlie Parker. The Beatles had come and gone—as a group—while he was still very much present in the music scene. This alone was worth celebrating, but the 1970s would turn out to be a difficult time for Davis.

Declining Health

The Miles Davis Quintet had never found a suitable replacement for John Coltrane. Davis had experimented with various saxophonists, but none stayed around long enough to make a major difference in the band's music. By 1972, it was nearly impossible to recognize the quintet. Most of the key members had left the group or died.

Davis remained as controversial a figure as ever during this challenging time, but his friends sensed that something was off. Sure, he played the trumpet passionately, but

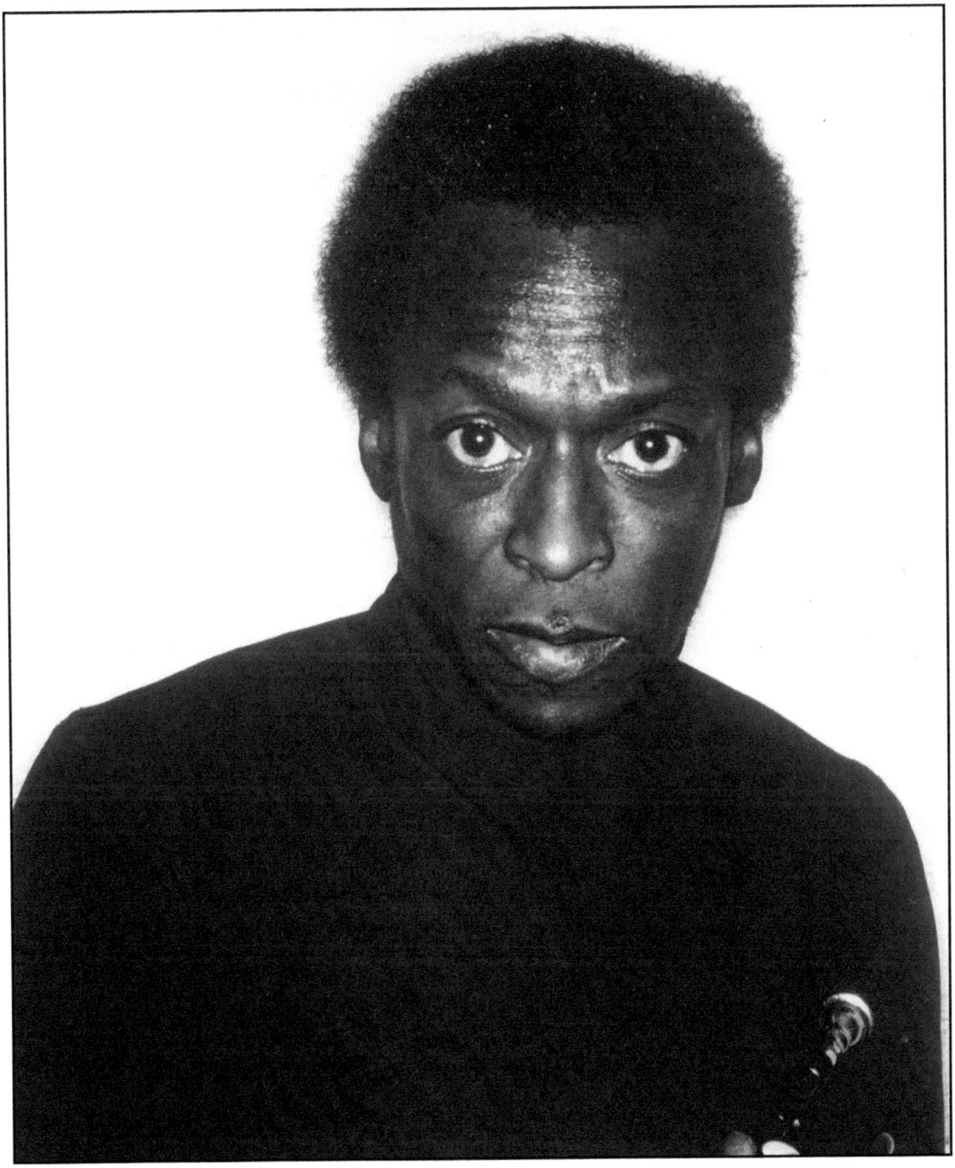

An aging Miles Davis poses for a portrait shot, circa 1973. The 1970s would be a difficult decade for the jazz trumpeter.

his performances began to take a toll on his body and mind. Increasingly, Davis described himself as being completely exhausted.

His past had finally caught up to him. His addictions to heroin and cocaine, refusal to slow down when he was ill, and medical conditions such as sickle-cell anemia, which he was diagnosed with a few years earlier, all contributed to his symptoms. In 1974, Davis was forced to rest after developing bleeding ulcers and pneumonia during a trip to Japan. To his dismay, the bout of pneumonia wouldn't be his last. After most of his major tours from then on, he contracted pneumonia, a side effect of his sickle-cell anemia.

In addition to pneumonia, Davis developed leg injuries so severe during a 1973 tour that he had to be airlifted home. And he faced financial difficulties as well as medical problems, which continued to plague him because of his use of drugs and alcohol. He considered retiring from music altogether in 1974 after he mixed a number of narcotics, both legal and illegal, with large quantities of vodka during a stop in São Paulo, Brazil. "When I got back to my hotel room, I thought I was having a heart attack," he recalled in his autobiography. "The band was scared; everyone thought I was going to die. I thought to myself, 'This is it.' But I pulled through that one."[1]

His narrow escape from death only led to more close calls. Addiction can make it difficult to muster up the strength to take better care of oneself, and it's nearly impossible to recover from a dependency on drugs without analyzing why one turned to substance abuse in the first place. Some people use drugs because they have undiagnosed mental

Sickle-Cell Anemia

While many of Miles Davis's health problems originated with his substance abuse, others, such as pain and exhaustion, stemmed from an inherited disease called sickle-cell anemia. At age forty-one, the musician was diagnosed with the incurable condition, which shortens one's lifespan.

Individuals with sickle-cell anemia lack enough normal red blood cells to distribute oxygen throughout their bodies. In healthy people, red blood cells are circular and can navigate blood vessels effortlessly. People with sickle-cell anemia, however, have red blood cells that are misshapen and can't move well. They get caught in small blood vessels, and this stops oxygen from traveling throughout the body as it should.

When oxygen isn't carried throughout the body, it leads to a host of symptoms, including chronic pain, fatigue, swelling of the hands and feet, and infections such as pneumonia, which Davis contracted numerous times.[2]

health problems. Others use them to numb themselves from emotional or physical pain. And a number of addicts have a genetic predisposition to substance abuse, meaning that drug and alcohol dependency runs in their family.

Several factors contributed to Davis's addictions, but arguably his greatest challenge was that few people in his

Music changed significantly during the 1970s. It saw the birth of punk music and bands like the Clash. Miles Davis didn't completely grasp all of the musical changes that occurred during this period.

Music Evolves

Popular music in the United States changed a great deal during the years Miles Davis left the industry behind. This was likely due, in part, to the deaths of people such as Jimi Hendrix, Janis Joplin, and Jim Morrison, all at the beginning of the 1970s. The Motown era, which had taken place from 1959 to 1972, had also ended.

As older genres of music shifted, newer forms gained momentum. Disco, punk, and hip-hop enjoyed mass popularity in the late 1970s. Artists such as Donna Summer, the Clash, Blondie, and the Sugarhill Gang all released popular singles during this time. In addition, a second "British Invasion" in rock seemed imminent, with English and Irish rock bands drawing fans from all over the world.

Miles Davis did not know what to make of these changes in music. In 1980, he found his return to music difficult, even strange.

circle felt comfortable telling him to get help. The musician was so successful at this point that no one could tell him what to do. His body, though, was sending him warning signs. In 1975, he had to pull out of a Miami concert because he felt too sick to perform. "By the time I cancelled, all my musicians and their equipment were already there and so the promoters of the concert kept all the sound equipment and tried to sue us," he recalled. "Right after this, I decided to quit."[3]

Taking a Break

By fall 1975, Miles Davis had dropped out of the music business. He felt physically and spiritually depleted and did not believe he had anything more to offer as a musician during this time. Still, he thought his exit from music would be brief, perhaps a year, tops. In the end, years went by before he returned to recording and performing music. He didn't even play his trumpet at home. What's worse is that he didn't use this time to work on himself. Instead, he continued to engage in self-destructive behavior. In his memoir, he explained:

> I didn't pick up my horn; for over four years, didn't pick it up once. I would walk by and look at it, then think about trying to play. But after a while I didn't even do that. It just went out of my mind because I was involved in doing other things; other things which mostly weren't good for me. But I did them anyway.[4]

This marked a huge shift for Davis, who had played his instrument almost constantly from the age of thirteen to forty-nine. Everything else in his life had always come second to music. He was so burnt out that he no longer felt inspired to play.

During his break from music, his drug and alcohol abuse continued, with Davis spending as much as $500 daily on cocaine. His apartment also became a wreck because he did not clean it or hire anyone to do so for him. Living in chaos led him to have a number of accidents around his home. The mess he'd made of his life wasn't limited to his apartment. Davis also had a string of affairs with various women, such a large number that he later confessed he could not remember their names. But an old friend, the actress Cicely Tyson, came back into his life, and they became a couple.[5]

Chapter 9

Comeback

Miles Davis married Cicely Tyson on Thanksgiving 1981. The ceremony took place at a western Massachusetts estate. Several of Davis's musician friends were present, and the event suggested a new beginning for the trumpeter.

A New Chapter

Tyson and Davis had known each other for nearly two decades before their nuptials, and the jazz musician expressed regret that he had not married the actress years earlier. He wed her around the same time that he'd returned to the recording studio. After years out of the music industry and without a wife, Miles Davis found himself with both his music and a committed partner again.

Extremely interested in health, Tyson was a positive influence for Davis. She persuaded him to alter his diet and get more exercise. She also motivated him to take a renewed interest in his music. But the marriage itself was troubled from the beginning. Davis cheated on Tyson with another woman less than a week after their wedding.[1] After several tumultuous years, it became clear that they needed to separate.

Cicely Tyson

Cicely Tyson was born in Harlem, New York City, on December 19, 1924 (though her birth year has also been listed as 1933). Her parents came from the Caribbean island of Nevis, and she grew up in a very religious household.

She was first a model and then an actress. At the start of her career, her family threw her out, believing that the entertainment industry was sinful. She and her family eventually reconnected. Although Tyson began acting in the 1950s, two decades would pass before she scored her breakout roles–in 1972's *Sounder* and 1974's *The Autobiography of Miss Jane Pittman*. She also appeared in a string of hit television shows, including *The Courtship of Eddie's Father*, *Mission: Impossible*, *Emergency!*, and the miniseries *Roots*. The winner of a Tony Award and three Golden Globes, she won an honorary Academy Award in 2018.

In the twenty-first century, Tyson's career is still going strong, with appearances opposite Viola Davis in the TV drama *How to Get Away with Murder* and film roles in various Tyler Perry productions. The actress also appeared in the hit 2011 film *The Help*.[2]

Actress Cicely Tyson and Miles Davis were a very stylish couple who had an extremely tumultuous relationship.

As Davis's marriage suffered, so did his public image. Throughout his career, Davis's relationship with the press had been rocky. His interviews with reporters often turned out to be contentious, and his 1989 interview with Harry Reasoner on the news program *60 Minutes* was no exception.

Initially, Davis didn't speak much during the interview. His voice had been soft and raspy for years, but many fans did not know that his vocal cords had been badly injured. They typically read his interviews in print publications such as *Rolling Stone* magazine. Interviewer Harry Reasoner did his best to draw Davis out, but his efforts mostly failed. For one, Reasoner insisted upon asking offensive questions, such as whether black musicians were genetically wired to be better at music than whites. He also asked if the pain of slavery somehow made African Americans more accomplished musicians.

Reasoner went on to discuss how Davis had kicked his heroin habit and then moved on to his alarming relationships with women. The musician was truthful about the role he played in the demise of his marriages. He admitted to unfairly blaming Cicely Tyson for many of his personal problems.

In response, Reasoner declared, "Miles Davis only does what he wants to do."[3] And some viewers agreed with him, while others though the interviewer had done a poor job posing questions to the jazz artist. The informal interview was scattered, with Davis directing where the conversation went. Reasoner concluded the piece by saying, "I don't know how I feel about Miles Davis."[4]

Feminist author Pearl Cleage speaks at the fourth annual National Book Club Conference in 2006. Cleage criticized Miles Davis's treatment of women.

In 1989, the year Davis sat down with Reasoner, the musician's memoir debuted. It was called *Miles: The Autobiography*, and it was written with Quincy Troupe. Published by Simon and Schuster, the memoir is uncensored. Essentially, the publisher allowed the jazz musician to use vulgar language and slang throughout the 448-page book. Fans appear to have enjoyed the autobiography, which is highly rated on sites such as Goodreads and Amazon.

But Miles Davis certainly had plenty of detractors, among them writer and feminist Pearl Cleage. In 1990, her book *Mad at Miles: A Blackwoman's Guide to Truth* was published. "He is guilty of self-confessed violent crimes against women, such that we should break his albums, burn his tapes, and scratch up his CDs until he acknowledges and apologizes and rethinks his position on The Woman Question," Cleage wrote in the book.[5] It was a rare counterpoint to Davis's image as a jazz god. To Cleage, the fact that Davis was one of the world's best musicians didn't absolve him of his crimes against women.

Years later, Davis's son Gregory would also write a book critical of the musician. The third child born to Miles and Irene Cawthon, Gregory lambasted his father in the book *Dark Magus: The Jekyll and Hyde Life of Miles Davis*. The book discusses Davis's drug abuse, sobriety, mood swings, and selfishness, and the happy times the family spent together as well. It came out in 2006.

Final Days

Just two years after Davis's autobiography debuted, the musician's health took a turn for the worse. He seemed to realize he was near the end. Physically, he was run down.

Members of Miles Davis's family, including his children Gregory (*center*) and Cheryl (*right*), accept the honor of Davis being inducted into the Rock & Roll Hall of Fame in 2006.

Mentally, he had good days but also poor ones. He made one last major appearance, at the Montreux (France) Jazz Festival in the summer of 1991. Traveling to the event led to yet another bout of pneumonia for him.

Time after time, Davis had escaped death. He had been hospitalized up to twenty times in the previous two decades. But his luck had run out. At sixty-five, he suffered a series of strokes and was put on life support for several days. Miles Dewey Davis died on September 29, 1991, in Santa Monica, California. He left behind his siblings and four children, three with his high school sweetheart, Irene Cawthon, and one with a woman named Marguerite Cantu.

Miles Davis was buried in New York City, fewer than 20 feet (6 meters) from the burial plot of Duke Ellington. After his death, accolades poured in from around the globe, with French newspapers offering kinder takes on Davis than their American counterparts. Jazz fans took his death particularly hard. While jazz greats such as Dizzy

What Killed Miles Davis?

In 1990, the average life expectancy for men in the United States was slightly more than seventy-five years old. At sixty-five, Miles Davis had died a decade younger. But what killed him? A number of medical conditions cut his life short.

Davis died at St. John's Hospital and Health Center in Santa Monica, California, and a hospital spokeswoman announced that pneumonia, respiratory failure, and a stroke had killed the musician.

The *Los Angeles Times* pointed out how these conditions were just the last of a long list of health problems for Davis. In addition to his drug addiction and throat operation for polyps, the trumpeter had endured hip surgery as a result of his sickle-cell anemia. He'd also suffered from gallstones, ulcers, leg infections, and broken bones.

The paper did not list sickle-cell anemia as a cause of death, but people with the disease have been found to have shorter lives than average.[6]

Gillespie, Billy Eckstine, and Cab Calloway were still alive at this time, many others had long ago died. Davis's death and the advanced age of the remaining jazz giants signaled the end of an era.

Chapter 10

Miles in Perspective

Miles Davis is remembered as a stellar jazz musician but a horrible person. In its obituary, the *Los Angeles Times* described him as "the trumpeter whose lyrical simplicity often reduced his audiences to tears but whose demonic habits sometimes overshadowed his genius for jazz."[1] "Demonic" may seem too harsh of a word for Davis, but the women in his life and his own children have painted similar portraits of him. In his memoir, the musician even discussed physically abusing actress Cicely Tyson.[2]

A Great Musician, a Flawed Person

Given how abusive and controlling Davis was, it comes as no surprise to learn that all of his marriages and serious relationships ended in divorce or separation. He was a deeply troubled person who did not seek the help that might have rescued him. During Davis's day, psychotherapy wasn't as commonplace as it is now, and children didn't learn about the effects of substance abuse in health class. He grew up during a time when little was known about the dangers of cigarette smoking. These circumstances don't let Davis off the hook for his behavior. They simply provide context.

After Davis's death, critics and fans not only debated what kind of person he was but also what his musical legacy would be. The press and the public debated whether he was the best trumpeter of his time and the top bandleader. Ever since he had recorded *Birth of the Cool*, Davis was recognized as the "coolest" of all jazz trumpeters. "Cool"

Domestic Abuse

Domestic violence takes a variety of forms; it is more than the physical abuse of a spouse, partner, or family member. It includes emotional abuse, such as name-calling, putdowns, and social isolation, making it difficult for the victim to see family and friends. It also includes economic or financial abuse, such as withholding money from the victim, accumulating debt in the victim's name, or interfering with the victim's education or employment.

Sexual abuse, stalking, or harassing someone are forms of domestic abuse as well.

Domestic abuse was a constant in the relationships of Miles Davis. He isolated the women in his life, accused them of infidelity while committing adultery himself, and slapped and hit them. But physical abuse goes beyond hitting; threatening to hurt victims and the people and pets they care about are examples as well. Throwing objects at someone, as Davis witnessed his mother do to his father, is a form of physical abuse, too. Rather than breaking the cycle of domestic violence, Davis continued it in his own intimate relationships.[3]

refers both to his stage presence and the spare musical structure he used. Once Davis was recognized in this way, he lived up to this reputation for decades. Only when *Bitches Brew* was released in 1970 did some people doubt that he was, indeed, the greatest, and coolest, jazz trumpeter.

Jazz fans don't agree about which trumpeter was the best. Dizzy Gillespie, from whom Davis learned a great deal, is widely considered the most talented trumpeter, while Davis is considered the smoothest one. Davis, after all, managed to engage listeners' senses and emotions with minimal variation in note and scale. But he lacked the power that Gillespie had on the trumpet.

How consistent Davis was as a musician also remains up for debate. In the recording studio, he was usually at the top of his game—on his trumpet and as a bandleader. But the road was a different story. Thousands of his fans can attest to his brilliance on certain nights and at certain clubs. Thousands of others can attest to how he underperformed on particular nights and at particular clubs. The road, of course, was challenging for Davis. He often abused drugs and alcohol and developed health problems such as pneumonia. Given this, his off nights weren't necessarily a sign of either his strengths or shortcomings as a musician. But excellent musicians often strive to be consistently great. Some of the top entertainers in the industry have been described as perfectionists. That didn't appear to be Miles Davis, at least not as his career progressed.

Miles Davis may not have steadily been the coolest jazz trumpeter, but most of the time his performances made him worthy of that distinction. In addition to cool, Davis was the most creative of the jazz giants. He showed

Pioneering hip-hop group Public Enemy, featuring Chuck D, is one of many acts that have been influenced by Miles Davis.

a willingness to experiment with different kinds of music, including flamenco, rock, and funk, in albums such as *Sketches of Spain* and *Bitches Brew*. He was clearly a risk-taker, and his willingness to be creative and experimental also earns him a spot on the short list of greatest jazz artists. Davis is almost totally responsible for establishing a new genre of jazz music, known as jazz fusion. Some critics believe that he was most creative during the 1980s, after his return to the music scene following a years-long hiatus.

Miles Davis's achievements are undeniable. He was one of the leading forces in jazz, bebop, funk, and fusion. The authors of *Brotherman: The Odyssey of Black Men in America* make a compelling case for the musician's greatness. They argue that no other artist could have influenced a group of musicians as eclectic as "Brian Eno, Parliament-Funkadelic, Prince, Public

Charlie Parker

Jazz saxophonist Charlie Parker was born August 29, 1920, in Kansas City, Kansas. When Parker was seven, he moved to Kansas City, Missouri, which had a wonderful music scene. He played the baritone horn in his school band but later discovered that he preferred the saxophone. He eventually left school to be a full-time musician.

In 1939, he decided to live in New York City. As his music career heated up, his personal life suffered. The saxophonist struggled with addictions to alcohol and heroin, and he also suffered from mental illness. He married three times in the 1930s and 1940s, but the relationships didn't last.

In 1945, Parker, nicknamed "Bird," became a bandleader for the first time and also performed with trumpeter Dizzy Gillespie, with whom he started a new form of jazz called bebop.

By the 1950s, Parker's career was in decline. His struggles with drugs led to bans by a number of New York City clubs. He attempted to take his life more than once but survived.

On March 12, 1955, Charlie Parker died from complications of long-term substance abuse. He was just thirty-four.[4]

Jazz musicians Wynton Marsalis and Miles Davis in New Orleans, Louisiana, on April 25, 1985. The men clashed when Marsalis questioned whether Davis was playing authentic jazz music.

Image Ltd., Talking Heads, Public Enemy, Living Colour, Marshall Jefferson, and Wynton Marsalis."[5]

Three decades after his death, Davis continues to inspire his fans. Actor Don Cheadle directed and starred in a 2016 movie, *Miles Ahead*, about his life. The way Davis dressed, his relationship with Cicely Tyson, and even his interviews garner interest from fans and non-fans alike. But how tragic his life was shouldn't be overlooked. How much more might he have achieved had he been able to control himself and treat the women and children in his life with the care and respect they deserved?

Chronology

1926

Miles Davis is born in Alton, Illinois.

1928

The Davis family moves to East St. Louis.

1929

The Great Depression begins.

1939

Davis receives a trumpet for his thirteenth birthday.
World War II begins in Europe.

1941

America enters World War II.

1944

Davis graduates from high school.
He arrives in New York to study at the Juilliard School.
He meets Dizzy Gillespie and Charlie Parker.

1949

Davis and his nonet record *Birth of the Cool.*
Davis plays at the first International Jazz Festival in Paris.
He meets Jean-Paul Sartre.

1950-1952

Davis becomes addicted to heroin

1953

He beats his addiction by going "cold turkey."

1955

Davis signs with Columbia Records, and producer George Avakian guides his career.

1957

Davis provides the music for French film *Lift to the Scaffold*.

1959

Davis and his group record *Kind of Blue*, considered one of the best jazz albums ever.

Three New York City policemen beat Davis.

He unsuccessfully sues the City of New York.

1961

Ebony magazine profiles Davis.

1968

Davis meets Jimi Hendrix, one of the few musicians he admires.

1969

The Woodstock Art and Music Festival takes place in upstate New York.

1970

Bitches Brew is released. New Miles Davis fans are thrilled. Older ones are appalled, even angry.

Jimi Hendrix dies.

1975

Davis goes into seclusion.

1980

He returns to the music scene.

1981

Davis marries actress Cicely Tyson.

1988

Davis and Tyson divorce.

1989

Harry Reasoner of *60 Minutes* interviews Davis.

1991

Davis dies in New York City.

The film *Dingo* is released. It features the last of Davis's music to reach the screen.

Chapter Notes

Chapter 1

A Prophet Without Honor

1. Mike Zwerin, ed, *Round About Close to Midnight: The Jazz Writings of Boris Vian* (New York: Quartet Books, 1988), p. 76.
2. Zwerin, p. 76.
3. Zwerin, p. 76.
4. Zwerin, p. 77.
5. Zwerin, p. 77.
6. Zwerin, p. 77.

Chapter 2

An Unhappy Childhood

1. "Robert Tanner Freeman," BlackPast.org, January 18, 2007, https://www.blackpast.org/african-american-history/freeman-robert-tanner-1846-1873/.
2. Miles Davis with Quincy Troupe, *Miles: The Autobiography* (New York: Simon & Schuster, 1989), p. 14.
3. Davis with Troupe, p. 11.
4. Davis with Troupe, p. 11.
5. Davis with Troupe, p. 28.
6. Davis with Troupe, p. 29.

Chapter 3

Jazz at a Crossroads

1. Miles Davis with Quincy Troupe, *Miles: The Autobiography* (New York: Simon & Schuster, 1989), p. 50.
2. Davis with Troupe, p. 50.
3. Davis with Troupe, p. 57.
4. Harry Reasoner, "Miles," *60 Minutes*, CBS, November 12, 1989, https://www.cbsnews.com/video/miles.
5. Harry Reasoner, "Miles."

Chapter 4

From Bop to Cool

1. Marc Crawford, "Miles Davis: Evil Genius of Jazz," *Ebony*, January 1961, p. 70.
2. Miles Davis with Quincy Troupe, *Miles: The Autobiography* (New York: Simon & Schuster, 1989), p. 76.
3. "Heroin," National Institute on Drug Abuse, June 2018, https://www.drugabuse.gov/publications/research-reports/heroin/what-are-long-term-effects-heroin-use.

Chapter 5

A Breakthrough Album

1. Miles Davis with Quincy Troupe, *Miles: The Autobiography* (New York: Simon & Schuster, 1989), p. 14.
2. Michael J. Agovino, "The Ensembles of Miles Davis Epitomized Cool," *New York Times*, March 11, 2016, https://www.nytimes.com/2016/03/13/fashion/mens-style/miles-davis-style-icon.html.
3. Agovino, "The Ensembles of Miles Davis Epitomized Cool."
4. Marc Crawford, "Miles Davis: Evil Genius of Jazz," *Ebony*, January 1961, p. 69.
5. John Szwed, *So What: The Life of Miles Davis* (New York: Simon & Schuster, 2002), p. 205.

Chapter 6

Top of the World

1. Miles Davis with Quincy Troupe, *Miles: The Autobiography* (New York: Simon & Schuster, 1989), p. 238.
2. Davis with Troupe, p. 238.

3. "John Coltrane Biography," Biography.com, April 2, 2014, https://www.biography.com/musician/john-coltrane.

Chapter 7
The Sixties

1. "Miles Davis Children, Wife, Biography, Net Worth, Death," Heightline, https://heightline.com/miles-davis-children-net-worth-death (retrieved April 19, 2019).
2. "Jimi Hendrix Biography," Biography.com, April 2, 2014, https://www.biography.com/musician/jimi-hendrix.

Chapter 8
Hard Times

1. Miles Davis with Quincy Troupe, *Miles: The Autobiography* (New York: Simon & Schuster, 1989) p. 330.
2. "Sickle Cell Anemia," MayoClinic.org, https://www.mayoclinic.org/diseases-conditions/sickle-cell-anemia/symptoms-causes/syc-20355876 (retrieved April 21, 2019).
3. Davis with Troupe, p. 331.
4. Davis with Troupe, p. 333.
5. Davis with Troupe, p. 336.

Chapter 9
Comeback

1. Miles Davis with Quincy Troupe, *Miles: The Autobiography* (New York: Simon & Schuster, 1989), p. 348.
2. "Cicely Tyson Biography," Biography.com, April 2, 2014, https://www.biography.com/actor/cicely-tyson.
3. Harry Reasoner, "Miles," *60 Minutes*, CBS, November 12, 1989, https://www.cbsnews.com/video/miles.

4. Reasoner, "Miles."
5. Pearl Cleage, *Mad at Miles: A Blackwoman's Guide to Truth* (Southfield, MI: The Cleage Group, 1990), p. 13.
6. Burt A. Folkhart, "From the Archives: Miles Davis, Jazz Legend and Innovator, Dies at 65," *Los Angeles Times*, September 29, 1991, https://www.latimes.com/local/obituaries/archives/la-me-miles-davis-19910929-story.html.

Chapter 10

Miles in Perspective

1. Burt A. Folkhart, "From the Archives: Miles Davis, Jazz Legend and Innovator, Dies at 65," *Los Angeles Times*, September 29, 1991, https://www.latimes.com/local/obituaries/archives/la-me-miles-davis-19910929-story.html.
2. Miles Davis with Quincy Troupe, *Miles: The Autobiography* (New York: Simon & Schuster, 1989), p. 366.
3. "What Is Domestic Violence?" The Center for Family Justice, https://centerforfamilyjustice.org/faq/domestic-violence (retrieved April 22, 2019).
4. "Charlie Parker Biography," Biography.com, April 2, 2014, https://www.biography.com/musician/charlie-parker.
5. Greg Tate, "Silence, Exile, and Cunning: Miles Davis in Memoriam," in *Brotherman: The Odyssey of Black Men in America*, ed. Herb Boyd and Robert L. Allen (New York: Ballantine Books, 1995), p. 666.

Glossary

analytical Thinking about something in a rational way; using logic or raising questions about something logically; picking a subject apart.

buoyant Cheerful or upbeat.

disillusioned Disappointed with someone or something; let down.

dysfunctional Describes an unhealthy way of relating to another person or situation; not behaving properly or as one should.

entitlement A feeling that one has the right to be treated in a special way or to break the rules.

inaugural The first or initial time an event takes place.

lament To mourn or express regret over something or someone.

nonet A musical group made up of nine people.

persevere To make it through a tough situation or time; to stick it out.

placate To give in to someone or please them to keep them satisfied or calm.

profound Something that is deep, intense, or very thought-provoking.

quarrel To argue or have a disagreement with someone.

refuge A safe place.

solace Peace or comfort, especially during a difficult time.

withdrawal A process in which the body develops a range of symptoms when a person stops using addictive substances.

Further Reading

BOOKS

Alkyer, Frank, ed. *The Miles Davis Reader: Interviews and Features from Downbeat Magazine*. New York: Hal Leonard Books, 2007.

Cook, Richard. *It's About That Time: Miles Davis On and Off the Record*. New York: Oxford University Press, 2007.

Long, Daryl. *Miles Davis for Beginners*. New York: Writers and Readers Publishing, 1992.

Maher, Paul, Jr., and Michael K. Dorr, eds. *Miles on Miles: Interviews and Encounters with Miles Davis*. Chicago: Lawrence Hills Books, 2009.

Nisenson, Eric. *The Making of* Kind of Blue*: Miles Davis and His Masterpiece*. New York: St. Martin's Press, 2000.

WEBSITES

Miles Davis

www.milesdavis.com

This is the musician's official website.

Miles Davis - The Rock & Roll Hall of Fame

www.rockhall.com/inductees/miles-davis

A biography of Davis on the Rock & Roll Hall of Fame website.

Index

Charlotte Etinde-Crompton

Samuel Willard Crompton

About the Authors

Charlotte Etinde-Crompton was born and raised in Zaire and came to Massachusetts at the age of twenty. Her artistic sensibility stems from her early exposure to the many talented artists of her family and tribe, which include master wood-carvers. She developed an interest in African American art after arriving in the United States.

Samuel Willard Crompton is a tenth-generation New Englander who now lives in metropolitan Atlanta. He was a history professor at Holyoke Community College for twenty-eight years. His interest in the arts comes from his wood-carver father and his oil-painter mother. Crompton is the author and editor of many books, including a number of nonfiction young adult titles with Enslow Publishing.